I Am a Hairdresser!

DISCOVER THE MAGIC OF HAIR

Lindsay O'Neil

I Am a Hairdresser!
Copyright © 2021 by Lindsay O'Neil

All rights reserved. No part of this publication may be reproduced, distributed, or transmitted in any form or by any means, including photocopying, recording, or other electronic or mechanical methods, without the prior written permission of the author, except in the case of brief quotations embodied in critical reviews and certain other non-commercial uses permitted by copyright law.

Tellwell Talent
www.tellwell.ca

ISBN
978-0-2288-5030-4 (Hardcover)
978-0-2288-5029-8 (Paperback)

I am a hairdresser!

"Like a fairy godmother,
I make your hair wishes come true!"

"While you fall asleep in my chair, I give your hair a warm and relaxing bubble bath"

I make long hair short

and short hair long!

"I make skinny hair look like lots of hair

and lots of hair look skinny!"

I make curly hair straight

and straight hair curly!

I make dark hair light

and light hair dark!

I can paint the colours of the rainbow!

I will turn a frown upside down.
I make smiles happen!

I will be more than your hairdresser.
I will be your friend!

With my skills and my talents, I make magic!
Some people confuse me for a magician!

I am a hairdresser! ☺

"Discover a story about the magic and possibilities of being a Hairdresser"

CPSIA information can be obtained
at www.ICGtesting.com
Printed in the USA
LVHW071908230621
690964LV00001B/31